To Father James McGuire S.D.B.

LONDON, NEW YORK, MELBOURNE,
MUNICH, AND DELHI

First U.S. Edition, 2001
This edition published in 2009 by DK Publishing,
375 Hudson Street, New York, New York 10014

A CIP record for this book is available from the Library of Congress.

ISBN 978-0-7566-5154-1

Printed and bound in China by L-Rex
Typeset in Monotype Old Style

see our complete product line at
www.dk.com

THE
CREATION
STORY

Illustrated by
NORMAN MESSENGER

DK Publishing

In the beginning God created the heavens and the earth. The earth was empty, a formless mass cloaked in darkness. And the Spirit of God was hovering over its surface.

Then God said, "Let there be light," and there was light. And God saw that it was good. Then he separated the light from the darkness. God called the light "day" and the darkness "night." Together these made up ONE DAY.

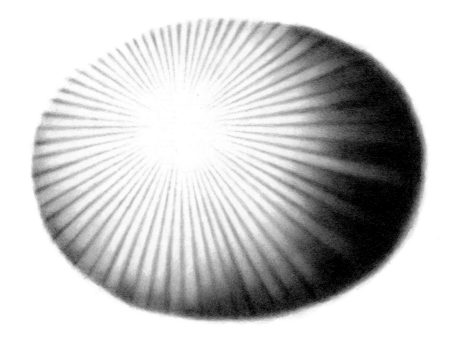

And God said, "Let there be space between the waters, to separate water from water." And so it was. God made this space to separate the waters above from the waters below. And God called the space "sky." This happened on THE SECOND DAY.

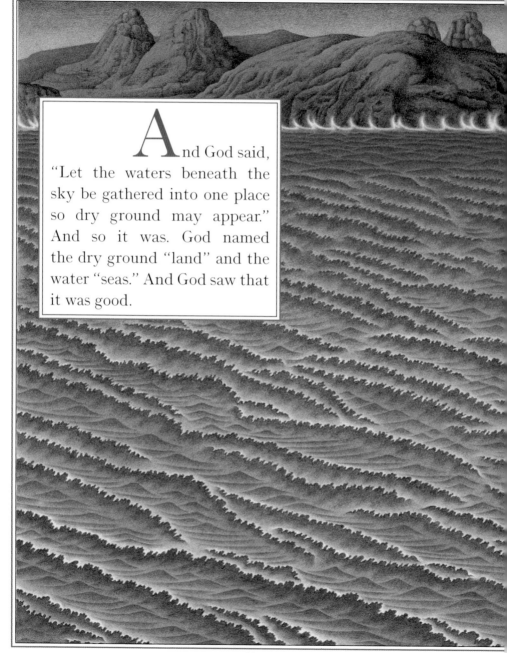

And God said, "Let the waters beneath the sky be gathered into one place so dry ground may appear." And so it was. God named the dry ground "land" and the water "seas." And God saw that it was good.

Then God said,
"Let the land burst forth
with every sort of grass and
seed-bearing plant."

"And let there be trees that grow seed-bearing fruit. The seeds will then produce the kinds of plants and trees from which they came." And so it was. And God saw that it was good. This all happened on THE THIRD DAY.

And God said, "Let bright lights appear in the sky to separate the day from the night. They will be signs to mark off the seasons, the days, and the years. Let their light shine down upon the earth." And so it was. For God made two great lights, the sun and the moon,

to shine down upon the earth. The greater one, the sun, presides during the day; the lesser one, the moon, presides through the night. He also made the stars. God set these lights in the heavens to light the earth. And God saw that it was good. This all happened on THE FOURTH DAY.

And God said,
"Let the waters swarm with fish
and other life."

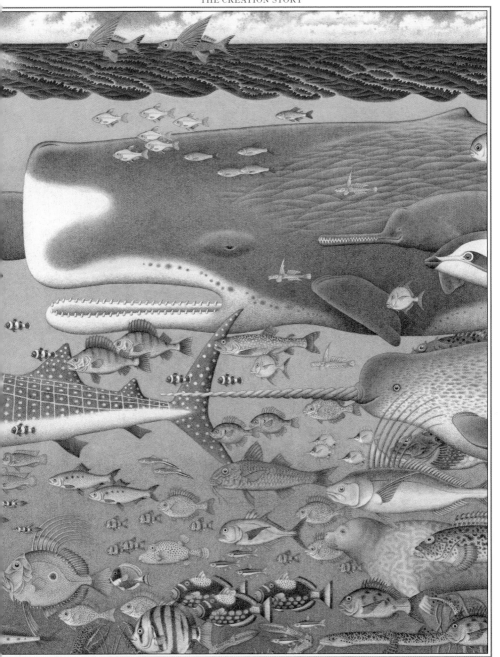

"Let the skies be filled with birds of every kind." And God saw that it was good. Then God blessed them, saying, "Let the fish multiply and fill the oceans. Let the birds increase and fill the earth." This all happened on THE FIFTH DAY.

And God said, "Let the earth bring forth every kind of animal—livestock, small animals . . ."

". . . and wildlife." And so it was. God made all sorts of wild animals, livestock, and small animals, each able to reproduce more of its own kind. And God saw that it was good.

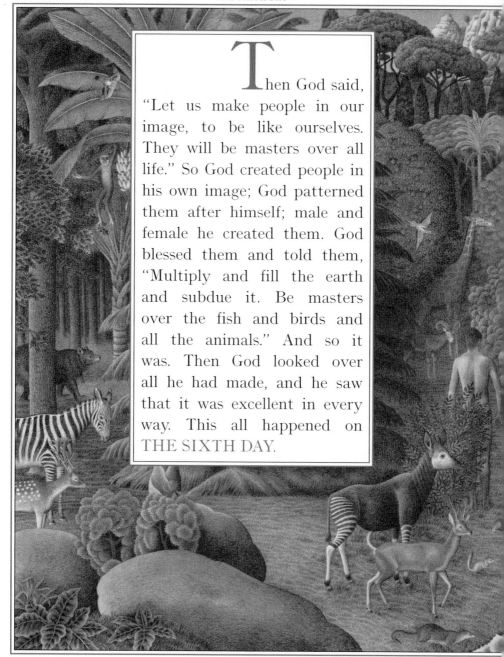

Then God said, "Let us make people in our image, to be like ourselves. They will be masters over all life." So God created people in his own image; God patterned them after himself; male and female he created them. God blessed them and told them, "Multiply and fill the earth and subdue it. Be masters over the fish and birds and all the animals." And so it was. Then God looked over all he had made, and he saw that it was excellent in every way. This all happened on THE SIXTH DAY.

So the creation of the heavens and the earth and everything in them was completed. On the seventh day, having finished his task, God rested from all his work. And God blessed THE SEVENTH DAY and declared it holy, because it was the day when he rested from his work of creation.